from

E

OOL

postcards.

Hayes

Feb 01

CENTRE
27-28 Dawson Way, St John's Shopping Precinct,
Liverpool, L1 1LH.

ISBN: 1 899181 47 4

Published by
Book Clearance Centre
27-28, Dawson Way
St. John's Shopping Precinct
Liverpool, L1 1LH,
Tel: 0151 708 5176.

Compiled by
Northern Publishing Service
28 Bedford Road
Firswood
Manchester M16 0JA
Tel: 0161 862 9399

Written By

Printed and bound by
Manchester Free Press
Longford Trading Estate
Thomas Street
Stretford
Manchester M32 0JT
Tel: 0161 864 5450

OTHER BOOK CLEARANCE CENTRES

Unit 2-8, Fishergate Centre, Preston, PH1 8HJ
Tel: 01772 884846
Unit 6, Marketgate Shopping Centre, Wigan, WN1 1JS
Tel: 01942 829499
Unit 28A, Town Square Shopping Centre, Oldham OL1 1XD
Tel: 0161 627 5244
27-28 Dawson Way, St. John's Precinct, Liverpool L1 1LH
Tel: 0151 708 5176
7, The Mall, Millgate Centre, Bury, BL9 0QQ
Tel: 0161 763 5700
Unit 47, The Concourse, Skelmersdale
Tel: 01695 557817
Market Walk, Chorley PR7 1DE
Tel: 01257 276799

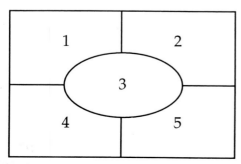

FRONT COVER PICTURES:
1. William Brown Street 1938
2. Parker Street, Owen Owens 1959
3. St. John's Gardens 1948
4. Plane spotting at Speke 1958
5. The Princess Landing Stage 1920

FOREWORD

By Billy Maher

"To be able to look back on one's past with satisfaction is to live twice." I read that phrase somewhere and it came to mind again as I looked through this superb collection of old postcards.

A postcard freezes that second in time and enables us to somehow get into the picture. How the memories came flooding back as I travelled down all those streets once more!

Listeners to my Sunday Show on BBC Radio Merseyside "BILLY MAHER — HIS MUSIC AND YOUR MEMORIES" will love this book. Everything is there. Old adverts, the opening of the Tunnels, Liverpool at war, the old bus routes, the Overhead Railway, the Airport and the Cathedrals. All are covered in over 130 pictures! With this collection of 100 years of postcards showing Old Liverpool, Cliff Hayes has done a marvellous job. In fact he's done us all a service!

Ta-ra-well.

INTRODUCTION

It is hard to imagine as fax's fly from business to business and home to home, car phones, and mobile phones screetch and bleep to keep busy people in contact, that only 100 years ago there was only two ways to get your message across. Go and see the person and tell them face to face (or messenger) or WRITE.

It is just over 100 years ago since the first postcard, plain, no picture, and with a printed stamp on was sent. Ordinary people who struggled to write letters could face a small card, and started to communicate. People left ready addressed cards (with the stamp printed on them) so that they could be informed of family happenings.

It was in 1894 the Post Office gave in to pressure from the publishers and allowed a photograph on one side of the card and a separate adhesive stamp, which was to be purchased from the Post Office, along with a small space for the communication. By the start of this century the address and message were finally allowed to be put on the back of the card together with a $1/2$d stamp, and the card was made larger (to its present size) and Britain was set for its postcard revolution.

Photography had passed its infancy, and was in full flow. It found a marvellous outlet in the postcard industry. In 1912 nine hundred million picture postcards were posted (yes, 900,000,000!) and about the same number were bought to add to the collections of people joining in this growing craze. The Post Office was much more dependable then, and the public posted with confidence. "I'll be home on the 10 a.m. train Saturday, please meet me" said a postcard posted on the Friday morning. With two and even three deliveries a day I have found cards posted at 8 a.m. on the way to work saying "Don't forget Mum I will not be home for tea tonight". In those days it was totally unthinkable that their message would not be delivered that day!!

It is thanks to these cards and the many small and large firms that produced them, that so much of our history from this century has been recorded and is available to us today. Celebrations, public ceremonies, disasters, accidents of one kind or another were faithfully recorded and turned into postcards, sometimes within hours of them happening.

The cards and photographs in this book are just some that I have gathered myself from many sources to give a fascinating glimpse into the past and to see what life was like in those

"Greetings from Olde Liverpool".

I hope you enjoy the book and that the memories brought back are pleasant ones.

ABOUT THE AUTHOR

Born 1945 and brought up in The Ball O'Ditton, Widnes, when it was proper and part of Lancashire. Educated at Chestnut Lodge Infants, Simms Cross Junior and then Wade Deacon Grammar School in Widnes, I then spent four years going to night school at The College of Art in Liverpool to study Printing, Design and English.

From the age of 13 I have been involved in printing, working part-time at a small local printers, then getting an apprenticeship at Swale Press (Widnes Weekly News, Runcorn, Liverpool etc.) then started helping and writing for Mersey Beat and also writing a disc and pop column for the Weekly News.

As youngest apprentice, one of my duties was catching the early H1 and meeting the delivery van at Garston at 5:35 every Wednesday morning, then spending 6½ hours delivering the Liverpool Weekly News to the shops of South Liverpool. This was when I first got to know the city.

Letchworth; Tinlings, Prescott: Ship's printer, Canadian Pacific to Canada and Cruising, Shaw Saville on Round-the-World trips and Japanese/Australian cruising etc.; Book production in Blackpool; newspaper works manager in the Isle of Man; Lino operator on National Newspapers (The Daily Mirror, The Sporting Chronicle, The Daily Telegraph etc.); computer training and twelve months as print salesman all added to a very broad view of every aspect of printing and of life in general.

Now settled in Manchester for the last twenty years, happily married with a teenage daughter. Cliff took up publishing five years ago and then progressed to writing books. This is the twelfth that he has edited or co-written, and the seventh in the series.

R865707

ACKNOWLEDGEMENTS

Cliff and Sylvia Hayes would like to thank Ted Gray for his help with the Liverpool Buses and Overhead Railway; Billy Maher for his support, and for writing the Foreword. John Glennard of Fennel Books, The Corn Exchange, Manchester for so much of the second-hand material; also, Catherine Rothwell for the Boat-Train picture and all friends in the book trade in Liverpool.

The cards in this book have come from my own collection, including 'Red Guides' and Official booklets of the past. If I have forgotten to credit any other source I apologise. Also, many thanks to Steve Coles for all his help and effort with the page layouts.

Thanks to Dorothy & Rob Greenley
for their faith and enthusiasm for putting this book back into print.

DEDICATION

This book is dedicated to the late Alf Hayes, my 'old man'. One-time Widnes' best barber, for all the times he took me around Liverpool as a kid. We rode the trams, the buses and the overhead. New Brighton was golden place and my parents took me there many times each summer - Thanks.

Let us get the argument out of the way. It is either LIVERPOOL coming from an old English word 'Liefer' meaning thick (as in soup or wallpaper paste) and Pool. So the name came from the murkey pool that was around the Paradise Street area.

But earlier this century they favoured another theory; that the Danes who lived on the Wirral and up the coast towards Formby referred to the area with two Danish words, Lide or Lithe meaning sea or creek/inlet by the marsh and although this theory is not in favour at the moment it is the one I like. The thought of the Danes over on the Wirral looking down on that area across the water and muttering about that awful place at the river mouth (bit like some of them today) appeals to my sense of humour.

Leverpoole, Liferpoole, Lyverpoole, Lyverpel, Liferpole; you will find all these spellings in documents of the past. Remember that scribes were given their instructions verbally and wrote roughly what they heard. Documents written about this time in London were written by people who had never heard the names of these Northern towns before, and made up their own spelling as they went along. Many towns and even cities have had their names changed forever by the guess of a clerk back in time

JOHN'S GARDENS & TUNNEL

LANDING STAGE

LORD ST. LIVERPOOL

GREETINGS FROM —LIVERPOOL—

MAIN ENTRANCE & GREAT PYLON LIGHT, MERSEY TUNNEL

DOCK BOARD OFFICE

The first mention of Liverpool was in a document from Prince John in 1192. As the 'Honour of Lancaster' John gave land along the river to Henry son of Howard de Wilden. John owned land near Preston but decided that if he were to have a go at the Irish he needed a port. He did not trust the Baron who owned the port at Chester and all the land around the river Dee. So in 1207 he swapped land that he had kept for hunting and falconry, near Preston, for land on the north bank of the River Mersey, where he could use the "Pool" for his men and ships. The name "Mersey" was first found in a document dated 1002 and means 'boundary'.

Liverpool was not important enough to get a mention in the Doomesday Book. West Derby got a mention along with six surrounding berewicks (plots) — it is thought Liverpool was one of them. West Derby ruled the area of Liverpool right up to the time in 1207 when John, now King John, issued his famous "Come and get some land 1/- a year" proclamation. It was read out by every Town Cryer in the land and it is estimated by the number of shillings paid that just under 200 families took up this offer, to enjoy all the privileges granted to freemen of the borough.

They came from West Kirby, they came from Chester and the Wirral, some came from further the north looking to be free men, and have two acres of land of their own. Borderers being persecuted, Geordies in a bit of lumber, young marrieds from north Lancashire looking for a start. That is how the mix of Liverpool started and they mixed in then and seem to have mixed in ever since.

CITY CENTRE

A postcard from the turn of this century. Central Station in all its glory. This station was the main link to Manchester in the 1940's and 1950's. The low square building on the left was the Cafe' (in the 1960's they did great a pie and chips for 2/6d).

The Exchange and Exchange Flags at Liverpool before the start of this century. The Flags was a great meeting place where business men would stroll and meet up with one another to exchange gossip and do deals.

St. George's Hall · Mersey Tunnel Entrance · THE CATHEDRAL LIVERPOOL · Victoria Memorial · Speke Airport

A great 1950's combination card of Liverpool. I always remember the Victoria Memorial as the place the trams went round in a circle.

Lime Street Station and the London & North Western Hotel looking down on the horse drawn omnibus. This picture from 1900.

Watch the pictures of the Anglican Cathedral as you go through the book. It has continued to be built throughout most of our lives. Pictures of the Cathedral or cards with the Cathedral on them are very easily dated because of the length of building time. See page 80

Hotels and Tariffs from 1930

Liverpool.

Midland Adelphi, Ranelagh Place : R. and b., fr. 17/- ; l., 4/6 ; t., 1/6 ; d., 7/6..
  Boarding terms : fr. 29/- per day.

Exchange Station, Tithebarn Street : R. and b., fr., 14/6 ; l., 4/6 ; t., 1/6.; d., 6/6.
  Boarding terms : fr. 25/6 per day.

North Western, Lime Street : R. and b., fr. 14/6 ; l., 4/6 ; t., 1/6 ; d., 6/6.
  Boarding terms : fr. 25/6 per day.

Angel, Dale Street.

Stork, St. John's Lane : R. and b., fr. 9/6 ; l., 2/6 ; d., 4/6.
  Boarding terms : 105/- per week ; 30/- per week-end.

Shaftesbury, Mount Pleasant : R. and b., fr. 8/6 ; l., 2/6 ; t., 1/6 ; d., 4/-.
  Boarding terms : 14/- per day.

Imperial, Lime Street : R. and b., single, 9/6 ; double, 17/- ; l., 2/6 ; t., 3/6 ; d., 5/-.

Washington, Lime Street.

Victoria, St. John's Lane : R. and b., 8/6.

Royal Court, St. John's Lane.

Clifton, 41 Islington.

Antrim, 73 Mount Pleasant : R. and b., 8/6.

Cook's Mona, St. John's Lane : R. and b., 8/6.

A very etheral card from 1905. A photograph, but looking like a painting. Note the cafe sign at roof height on the right. Lord Street, busy and bustling in 1905. Most of these buildings were destroyed during the War.

Parker Street 1946. Finding this street was quite a job. It is the small street between Church Street and Clayton Square. Elliott Street is the street from Clayton Square up to Lime Street (now partly pedestrianised, with the Welcome Centre on the corner).

LIVERPOOL.

The Landing Stage, Liverpool.

A lovely combination card well worth
a closer study. The Cathedral minus
its tower. All three buildings on the
front and the St. Tudno at the landing
stage date these pictures to 1925-
ish, although the card was not posted
until Easter 1927.

LIVERPOOL, ST. JOHN'S GARDENS.　　　　　　　　V5121

A 1948 postcard of St. Johns gardens below St. George's Hall. Just in case you are wondering why it is not called St. George's Gardens, it takes its name from St. Johns Church which stood here from 1783 for 115 years. When the graveyard was converted into a park it was unkindly nicknamed "The Stone Yard." There are ten statues in this small park including a South African War Memorial to the Liverpool Regiment. It is well worth going to see these statues of prominent Liverpudlians, all well known for their philanthropy, and their work with the poor and needy. See if you can find the plaque to the French prisoners who died in custody in Liverpool from the Crimean War.

LIVERPOOL, LIME STREET.　　　　　　　　V5128

A good view of Lime Street in the 1950's. The buildings on the right were cleared in the 1960's. Lime Kiln Road (named after the lime burning which took place on the spot where the station is now). Later shorted to Lime Road, then Lime Street.

Another card from the 1950's showing Dale Street taken from the front of the Town Hall looking towards the tunnel.

LIVERPOOL

ENTRANCE TO MERSEY TUNNEL FROM MUSEUM STEPS

ST. GEORGE'S HALL AND LIME STREET

PETER PAN STATUE SEFTON PARK

LIVER BUILDING, DOCK OFFICE AND CUNARD BUILDINGS

LIVERPOOL CATHEDRAL

A charming composite card, but very hard to date. The Cathedral is into the 3rd stage of building, so it is after 1949. The St. George's Hall picture has horse drawn vehicles in it and 1920's dress on the pedestrians. I like the Peter Pan statue from Sefton Park in the centre.

LIVERPOOL, LOOKING DOWN WILLIAM BROWN STREET TOWARDS TUNNEL ENTRANCE.   V5133

The captions says it all. A 1938 card. The building on the right is the Picton Reading Rooms named after Sir James Picton. He was chairman of the Libraries & Museums Committee for over 25 years and laid the foundation stone on his 70th birthday in 1875. Scousers love nick-names and this one revelled in "Pictons Gasometer" when opened in 1879. Also a good shot of the Steble Fountain built in 1879. The four statues at the base of the fountain represent the four seasons.

St. George's Hall, Liverpool

A 1910-ish card showing St. George's Hall, a good picture with few people and no traffic in it. St. George's Hall itself is a strange mixture which only came about by accident. In 1836 a need was felt for a building to host the famous Three Day Music Festival, but also a building that could be used for Civic Balls and Functions. In typical Scouse style, they laid the foundation stone, and then held a competition for a design for the Concert Hall. Harvey Longsdale Elmes a 23-year-old rising architect won the competition with a classic Gredco — Roman style building. At the same time the Law & Order Committee were planning a new Law Court and a year later they too had a competition for a new Law Court, and guess who won ... yes, the young Mr Elmes.

As the cries of "its a fiddle" died down the Corporation asked him to put the two buildings into one and in 1842 work started on the unlikely combination of Law Courts and Ballroom! Sadly Elmes worked too hard and fell ill. His doctor said that he needed a sea trip and a rest in Jamaica, so off he went, but died when he arrived there in December 1847. A name worth remembering next time you pass the Hall, 'Harvey Elmes' a young man who at 26 had the vision to plan this truly great building and who in his own fathers words was "a martyr to architecture." The hall opened in Septemnber 1854 but even then it had its critics. One criticism was that the Jury Room had no toilet. But 50 years later a local lawyer was heard to admit that this had probably helped make justice move faster.

Looking down Castle Street at the Town Hall. It is hard to imagine that where the buildings on the left are, there was once a 9ft thick and 26ft high stone wall, and where those gents are crossing the road was a moat! The Castle was built in the early part of the 13th century and finally cleared in 1726 some five hundred years later.

SHIPPING AT PRINCES STAGE

THE WATERFRONT

THE CATHEDRAL

GREETINGS FROM LIVERPOOL

THE CENTRAL LIBRARY, WILLIAM BROWN STREET

ENTRANCE TO MERSEY TUNNEL

A composite card from just before World War II. Well worth a closer study. Two liners at the landing stage (the far one looks like Canadian Pacific line). The tunnel entrance is only just opened and has toll booths at this side as well. The picture labelled clearly The Central Library is of course not that but the William Brown Museum next door.

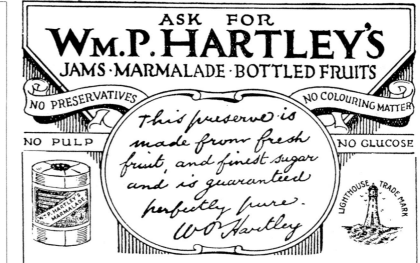

A card from 90 years ago looking up Lord Street towards Church Street at the top. Open top trams and horse drawn cabs reflect an opulent Edwardian Liverpool.

The Town Hall shown here in about 1904. This is the third Town Hall on this site and was built in the 1750's. It has survived quite a few disasters including a seamens' attack in 1775; an attempted blowing up in 1881 and bombing during the blitz in June 1941.

Looking up Bold Street, Liverpool.   J. K. & Co., L'pool. Copyrig

A very early postcard from the time when you had to write on the front. How uncluttered this square and street was in this picture from about 1895. The spot this picture was taken from is actually called Waterloo Square named after the Waterloo Hotel which stood where Central Station once was. The Waterloo Cup also got its name from this Hotel. The Lyceum Gentlemens Club on the left was built around 1803 and also contained the Liverpool Library. Next time you stop and buy flowers from the stalls which stand where the horse-drawn cab is, have a closer look at this building, and imagine when it was THE meeting place for the ship owners and merchants of the city.

The Cenotaph outside the St. George's Hall. Unveiled 12 years after the end of the First World War by the Earl of Derby. It is one of the few 1914-18 memorials that were not added to by the fallen of the Second World War. The bronze on this side depicts "The Mourners Left Behind" while the other side shows "The Soldiers Who Fought".

Looking across the Plateau towards The Empire Theatre. You know of course that the Column on the left has 'The Iron Duke' Wellington, standing up on top and rumour has it that the statue was made from the cannons captured at the battle of Waterloo. The lions were originally at each end of the Hall, one pair looking north and the other pair looking south. But they were moved (some job) when St. John's Lane, opposite Lime Street Station entrance, was widened. The Empire Theatre had probably just been rebuilt in this card from around 1930.

Empire Theatre, Lime Street, Liverpool.

LANDING STAGE AND DOCKS.

HUSKISSON DOCK & S.S. CARONIA

DOCK BOARD OFFICES

LIVERPOOL

LIVERPOOL CATHEDRAL.   201861 J.V.

ST. GEORGE'S SQUARE.

A 1935 card and the Cathedral looking very bare. Can you make out the New Brighton Tower on the skyline in the left hand corner of the Landing Stage picture?

GOOD LUCK from

LIVERPOOL

LIVERPOOL CATHEDRAL

ENTRANCE TO MERSEY TUNNEL FROM MUSEUM STEPS

MERSEY SIDE

PIER HEAD AND MERSEY SIDE

A Wartime card with a cheering rallying message on the back from the Prime Minister. Hundreds of these cards were sent by visiting sailors etc., calling at the Port.

EXCEL SERIES

POST CARD

FOR CORRESPONDENCE

"This is the time for everyone to stand together, and hold firm."

—The Prime Minister.

PRINTED IN ENGLAND

FOR ADDRESS ONLY

A view of the back of St. George's Hall showing William Brown Street and St. John's Gardens. Just after this picture was taken work was started on the Mersey Tunnel. Maybe they had already started digging in those underground toilets in the foreground.

A nice picture of Victoria's Monument in St. George's Square. I always remember this Square as being the boarding point for the trams and buses up to the match

The Custom House with its Gothic front and wonderful dome. Sadly this building was completely destroyed during the War but stood opposite the exit to Albert Dock.

St. George's Hall in 1920. The lions having just moved and St. John's Road widened. The total cost of this building is one of those figures easy to remember it was £333,330. including furnishings and carpets.

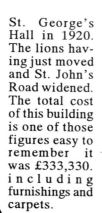

The North Western Hotel and Empire Theatre in about 1928. The Cenotaph has not yet been put in place.

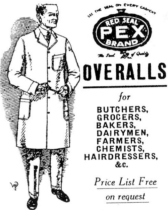
The Walker Art Gallery with the statues of Michael Angelo and Raphael on either side of the entrance steps.

Shewing Castle Street over 120 years ago with our premises at No. 3.

PENLINGTON & BATTY

DIAMOND MERCHANTS
and JEWELLERS

Established 1819

Late 2 & 3 St. George's Crescent, Castle Street

TEMPORARY PREMISES :

c/o ROBINSON, BATTY & Co.,

19 TEMPLE STREET (opposite Fruit Exchange),

Victoria Street   -   -   **LIVERPOOL, 2**

Owing to the "civilizing" influences of the Hun we regret to say that after 122 years trading the above Liverpool premises are no more.

Not least of the many trials imposed by War is the restriction and limitation of supplies.

Better days will come and bring with them normal trading conditions.

In the meantime we assure you as always of our personal service within the limits imposed by authority.

Also

W. BATTY & SONS LTD., 25 KING ST., MANCHESTER, 2

An interesting advert from the Liverpool Year Book of 1943 with the company regretting they have had to move. I like the wording "civilizing influences of the Hun". Though I know the caption can't really be right. It would make the picture 1820, a little early for pictures of this quality.

1943 . . . CITY CENTRE
(and trying to be business as usual)

for Fashions, Fabrics
and Furnishings
of Quality

Wm. Henderson & Sons Ltd.
Church Street, Liverpool, 1.

Three postcards from 1930 from Valentine & Sons Ltd., made to sell to the students arriving at the new University of Liverpool. Left, the Victoria Buildings; top, Arts Building and the right one is the Chemical Laboratory.

You can see what the Philharmonic Hall looks like today but here is a postcard of the old Philharmonic which was destroyed by fire in July 1933 after standing for 80 years. No time was lost in replacing it with its now equally famous successor.

LIVERPOOL PHILHARMONIC ORCHESTRA

Leader : HENRY DATYNER

Conductor
SIR MALCOLM SARGENT

Soloist
EDWIN FISCHER

EIGHTH
TUESDAY SUBSCRIPTION CONCERT
20th DECEMBER 1949
at 7 p.m.

A lovely shot of the famous Pirate Ship in Sefton Park. Can you make out the Peter Pan statue just behind it? Recently, when the Tall Ships were in, a miniature Galleon gave trips around Albert Dock, to the delight of many youngsters. Imagine the years of delight that the Galleon in Sefton Park gave at 6d a ride.

Pirate Ship, Sefton Park, showing Peter Pan.

An early postcard of Sefton Park and its bridge. Posted in September 1904 to add to Doris's growing collection.

Sefton Park.

Liverpool.

The Aviary in Sefton Park. Built to add to the delight of strolling round this green oasis. Card from about 1911.

The Aviary, Sefton Park, Liverpool

Children's Gardens, Sefton Park.

Staying with Sefton Park — and an after the Second World War postcard showing the Children's Gardens with the fairy tale figures and gnomes.

THE "PALS" BARRACKS, PRESCOT. NO. P. 13.

PUB. BY
J. EDWARDS, PRESCOT.

SMITHDOWN ROAD. LIVERPOOL.

A real memory jerker this one. A postcard from around the time of the First World War showing the barracks of the 'Liverpool Pals' in Prescot. Locally published by J. Edwards of Prescot. I can imagine this one being sent home by many newly enlisted squaddies.

Smithdown Road before the Second World War and the shop blinds are down and the busy area is ready for another day.

Grave of the Child of Hale. Hale nr. Liverpool.

Outings and trips formed the high-light of many a Societies year. Here is a 1904 postcard showing the grave of the Child of Hale at Hale Church. Sent back to Anglesey from N.W. enjoying the Church Choirs picnic at Hale Lighthouse.

A nice view of Knowsley Hall from the Gardens about 1948. Knowsley Hall was the home of the Earls of Derby the family so closely connected with Liverpool.

WEST DERBY

A set of West Derby postcards published around 1925 showing the newly built and modernised housing estates and road layouts. Most speak for themselves.

Queen's Drive, West Derby showing St. Matthews Catholic Church on the left and St. Andrew's Church on the right.

Holly Lodge High School, West Derby 1920's. Now Holly Lodge Comprehensive School Upper.

Queen's Drive again at the corner of Muirhead Avenue with the policeman singing 'I took myself on point duty but nobody asked me to play'.

Muirhead Avenue in the 1920's. Again bereft of traffic except for the solitary parked car.

Two fine views of Lark Hill Gardens in West Derby. Built to bring a little greenery to the middle of a housing estate.

THE BRIDGE, LARKHILL GARDENS, WEST DERBY.

THE LAKE, LARKHILL GARDENS, WEST DERBY.

BOWLING GREENS, MUIRHEAD GARDENS, WEST DERBY.

The other gardens in the area were Muirhead Gardens with its recreation facilities including bowling green and tennis courts.

THE MANSION, MUIRHEAD GARDENS, WEST DERBY.

Two cards one showing the bowling greens in use by the ladies, and the other showing the fine Mansion House in the grounds.

MILLBANK, QUEEN'S DRIVE, WEST DERBY.

Liverpool started off as just an off-shoot of West Derby but in 1928 finally got its revenge by absorbing West Derby U.D.C. into the City of Liverpool.

One last look at West Derby and the corner of Queen's Drive and Mill Bank towards West Derby road.

Three good post-cards of the Promenade just after it opened in 1933. Part of the filled-in area later became the Garden Festival site.

When the digging of the Mersey Tunnel started in 1930 one of the problems was what to do with all the soil, clay and rocks taken out. Then someone hit on a bright idea, why not take the debris to Otterspool where there was already a land fill project using the City's rubbish. The clay and soil from the tunnel was used to seal and solidify the area. That is how Liverpool came by Otterspool Promenade!

Otterpool promenade just completed

SPEKE HALL

The north front of Speke Hall taken about the time of the First World War.

Speke Hall is definitely one of the oldest buildings in the district and is a famous example of a black and white mansion. The Hall was started in about 1490 with 1598 written over the principle entrance and 1605 carved into the South Garden gate. Home of the Watt family up until 1921 when it was left on the death of Adelaide Watt to trustees. It was later leased to Liverpool Corporation and is now the property of the National Trust.

Another fine card of
the Hall in 1925.

Calderstone Park in
1928. The Stones
themselves have been
moved, but the Park
is still a great place
to stretch your legs.

The gardens are still there, and there is toilets and a cafe there.

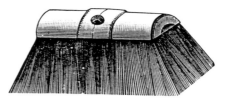
46

I found this description of Childwall in a 1930's Guide to the City. Amazing that the area could be described as favoured by vocalists!

The House at Childwall in 1919

One of the birth places of Methodism in Liverpool 'The Old Brunswick' as it was nicknamed. Built around 1810.

A fine day in the late 1950's sees plane spotters and visitors on the terraces at the old airport off Speke Boulevard.

In 1950 when this photograph was taken this was an exciting and modern card showing the latest in air transport (no doubt lined up just for the picture). It was always exciting on the H1 or H20 bus going past the airport as the planes were dragged out by tractors and pushed into place for take off.

PIER HEAD

St. George's Dock and the water front just before it was filled in. Liverpools' water front was becoming increasingly crowded and the ships using the docks were getting larger. Liverpool decided on a bold plan to fill in one of the older and smaller docks and build in its place some fine buildings. The turn of the century saw the filling in of George's Dock and 1904 saw the start of the building of what was offically known as 'The Offices of the Mersey Docks and Harbour Board'.

The newly completed Dock Board Offices, in all its fine glory and splendour. Started in 1904 and costing £250,000 it is a magnificent building. The inside should really be seen to appreciate what a grand building it is. Shortened names and even nicknames were allowed for telegrams, I like the Docks & Harbour Board telegram address "NEPTUNE LIVERPOOL".

210   ROYAL LIVER BUILDINGS AND DOCK OFFICES, LIVERPOOL.

Take a close look at this 1913
postcard from W.H.S. Mersey
Series, see if you know what's
missing. Yes it's the Cunard
Building in the middle. For some
reason they built the Dock Offices,
and when they were completely
finished they started on the
foundations of the Liver Building.
Then when that was fully finished
in 1912 and Cunard building was
started 1914 this must be a 1913
picture. Maybe they didn't know
if the filled in dock would take
the weight so they built slowly,
one by one.

OVERHEAD RAILWAY, LIVER BUILDINGS AND DOCK OFFICES, LIVERPOOL

A 1950 card showing the Tunnel vent building and the Overhead Railway in clear shot.

The Dock Board Offices. Again just after it opened for business in 1907. There was a lot of arguments about the money being spent on the dome and fine furnishing. One board member argued that "It was not the duty of the Board to beautify the town". Luckily the others did not agree and the dome went ahead.

Royal Liver Buildings, Liverpool.

The Clock in the Liver Building was designed and constructed by Gent & Co., Ltd., and they had this card printed in 1913 to show off that fact. Did you know that the dial was bigger than 'Big Ben's' and it was the largest electrical turret clock in England, no? Well you do now.

ROYAL LIVER BUILDING, LIVERPOOL.

Length 301 feet ; width 177 feet ; height, ground to top of Liver Birds, 322 feet ; height of Birds 18 feet ; number of floors (including six in each tower) 17 ; number of lifts 17 ; number of steps (basement to tower) 483.

The Clock, which is the largest Electric Turret Clock in England, was designed and constructed by Messrs Gent & Co.. Ltd., of Leicester. Diameter of dials 25 feet (2½ feet wider than those of "Big Ben") ; weight of clock mechanism 4 tons ; weight of four pairs of hands (with bearing spindles) 2 tons.

Two names that would go down in history caught together in 1910. The Liver Buildings, during construction, and the Royal Mail Ship 'Lusitania' about to leave on an Atlantic crossing.

The three buildings complete at last, making up what is now one of the most recognisable skylines in the world. Today it is hard to think of them ever being separated. Maggie sent this card to Nellie in about 1925, telling her what a lovely holiday they were having in Liverpool! "Been over a big liner the Montclare" she writes. The Montclare sailed on her maiden voyage from Liverpool on August 28th 1924 and continued in service with Canadian Pacific until the war.

An aerial view from 1950 There are still some big gaps in the cities buildings due to the bombing during the War. One thing this postcard shows very clearly is that the Cunard Building, that was built last, had to be designed to fit in! You can see how much narrower it is at the front than at the back. There is in fact more than 20ft difference.

They didn't take a lot of care about the captions (this card was issued by a southern firm). It makes it sound as if the three were all the Royal Liver Buildings. Never mind. Did you know that the Liver Birds are 18 feet high. And did you know that there are seventeen stories in the Liver Building, including six in the towers.

LIVERPOOL, MERSEY AND ROYAL LIVER BUILDINGS.

This is how I remember the Pier Head. Liverpool Waterfront in 1952 (40 years ago). Three covered gang ways going down to the Landing Stage. The excitement of the movement while you were walking down. Guessing if it would be almost level (high tide) or a really steep angle and you would have to hold tight to your dad's hand.

Landing Stage, Liverpool

Snow on the Landing Stage. This is an unusual card, taken in 1903 and it was sold in thousands in the winter of 1904. It was the first time that cards were allowed to have the whole of the front for the picture, with the message on the back. Snow was faked by using bleach on the negative on many Edwardian cards, but this one seems to be genuine.

THE LIVERPOOL & NORTH WALES STEAMSHIP COMPANY LTD.

DAILY SAILINGS
(SUNDAYS INCLUDED)
WHITSUNTIDE TO SEPTEMBER

From PRINCES LANDING STAGE, weather and other circumstances permitting

SUBJECT TO ALTERATON WITHOUT NOTICE

"ST. TUDNO" or "ST. SEIRIOL"

Leaving		each day		Leaving		each day
LIVERPOOL		10 45 a.m.		MENAI BRIDGE		3 45 p.m.
LLANDUDNO	} due	1 5 p.m.		LLANDUDNO	} due	5 0 p.m.
	} dep.	1 15 p.m.			} dep.	5 15 p.m.
MENAI BRIDGE	due	2 40 p.m.		LIVERPOOL	due	7 40 p.m.

N.B.—Passengers for Bangor, Beaumaris and Anglesey Resorts—
Crosville Bus Service from Menai Bridge

A 1946 postcard showing a full Landing Stage and a ferry heading across the River. I wonder why so many of the ferries of the Mersey take their names from flowers. We all remember the Iris, and the Daffodil (renamed 'Royal' Iris and Daffodil after World War I because of sterling service). But did you know there was also a 'Crocus' and a 'Rose' as well as a 'Thistle, 'Pansy' and 'Daisey'.

WHITE STAR LINE

Liverpool Waterfront

11456

A very full Gladstone Dock during the Seamans Strike in the 1960's. The Empress of Canada and the Empress of England on the left and a collection of Blue Funnel boates on the right.

The Empress of England was 25,585 ton and 640 ft long. It did the trans-Atlantic run from Liverpool to Quebec, (a twelve day round trip) and pictured here on the St. Lawrence River, Quebec in 1958 showing her old C.P. colours.

Cunard and Canadian Pacific were the two largest companies in Liverpool for passenger liners after World War Two. This was my ship 'Empress of England'. For seven years she did not move without me on board.

The funnels of C.P. ships carried a chequered flag up to 1962, then they started changing them to this crescent design. In 1970 this ship was sold to Shaw Saville and renamed the Ocean Monarch, so this postcard is from around 1965.

This is a picture of the Ocean Monarch, and you would be forgiven for thinking that this picture was taken somewhere really exotic, when in actual fact it was taken at Tranmere Oil Terminal with Cammell Laird workers still on board putting the finishing touches to the refit in July 1971. This is just one of the hundreds of huge ocean liners that once used to come Liverpool, and sadly no more.

One of the ships mentioned in the Cunard advertisement R.M.S. Lucania moored in the Mersey with her launch alongside to take passengers ashore. This card from 1905 and the famous skyline has not yet started to be built. You can just make out Our Lady and St.Nicholas's (The Sailor's Church) on the right hand side.

The last ship built for the Liverpool run 'The Empress of Canada'. The third ship to bear this name, it was commissioned in 1959 and built to replace Canada II which caught fire in Gladstone Dock on 25th January 1953 and was completely destroyed.

Liverpool made quite a fuss when the QE 2 called and I even went down to see her. But only 30 years ago you could find four or five big liners in the River. Sometimes there wasn't even room for them at the Landing Stage and would have to start unloading on to the ferries or launches.

Two cards showing the river and the tugs. There were two companies, the Liverpool Screw Towing Company with their 'Cock' Tugs, Pea Cock, Flying Cock, Heath Cock etc., and their distinctive blast 'Cock-a-doodle-doo' (one long and four short blasts) and the Alexandra Tugs.

The ships had a great social life. Here is the football team and officials off the 'England' pictured here after winning the 'Montreal Cup' and other silverware in 1969. I wonder if Peter, Robbie and any of the others are still around. (I'm the 7th from the left, back row). We played football in Tokyo, Fiji, New Zealand and Singapore amongst other countries.

The Princes Landing Stage in about 1930. Up until 1934 when the tunnel opened, there were two car ferries from this spot over to Birkenhead and Wallasey. The alternative to this was a 40 mile drive and the Transporter at Widnes or the 60 mile drive round to Warrington. The ship at the back looks like the 'Duchess of Bedford' (renamed 'Empress of France' at the start of the War) but I can't quite make out the name on the ship at the front.

Many Liverpudlians found work on the liners and hundreds of postcards like this one found their way back to the mantlepieces of many a home around Liverpool. This picture of the 'Empress of Scotland' at Quebec with the Chateau Champlain behind. This ship was once called 'Empress of Japan' in 1930 and sailed the Pacific, but at the outbreak of the War it was renamed 'Empress of Scotland'. It was sold to a German company in 1958 and finished up as the 'Hanseatic'.

EMPRESS OF SCOTLAND. (2).

CANADIAN PACIFIC 'EMPRESS OF BRITAIN' - TOURIST COCKTAIL BAR

These liners were the pride of Liverpool and Liverpool lads kept them spick and span. They were very solid and dependable, no tubular steel, no plastic. The first-class Club Room on the 'England' was just as you would have imagined a Gentlemans Club in 1900 to be; winged back chairs, two inch thick carpets, and personal service by only the most senior of stewards.

The Tourist Class Cocktail Bar on the 'Empress of Britain' and the Tourist (C.P. did not say Second Class) Smoking Lounge on the 'Empress of England'.

THE CANADIAN PACIFIC SHIPS

Empress of Scotland

Empress of Britain (II)

Montrose

Empress of Australia

Beaverdale

Empress of England

Duchess of Bedford as Empress of France (II)

Empress of England (III)

DOMAIN of NEPTUNUS REX

To all Sailors wherever ye may be
to all subjects of the Realm of the Raging Main; to all Sharks and Swordfish and other Finny Folk; to all Sea Serpents and Whales; to all Mermaids, Naiads, Sirens and Luring Beauties of the Bays

Greeting ★ KNOW YE that on this TWENTY-SIXTH day of MAY 1970 of the on board the Good Ship OCEAN MONARCH

SHAW SAVILL LINE

in Latitude 0° 00' 0' and Longitude............ in the PACIFIC Ocean

Cliff Harper

attempted, without due authorisation or making the customary obeisance, to enter the Royal Domain of His Oceanic Majesty, and was accordingly subjected to the TRIAL AND INQUISITION OF THE FATHOMLESS DEEP

Whereas the said intruder having endured these Ordeals with Courage and Fortitude, H.F. is now deemed worthy by His Majesty to be numbered as ONE OF HIS TRUSTY SHELLBACKS

Wherefore WE, DAVY JONES, Viscount Atlantis, Baron of the Boundless Seas, etc., etc., His Majesty's Principal Scribe,
REQUEST AND REQUIRE in the Name of His Majesty, Neptune, Ruler of the Mighty Oceans, all those whom it may concern to allow the bearer to pass freely without let or hindrance and to afford every assistance and protection to which he is entitled by virtue of this FREEDOM OF THE RAGING MAIN.

Davy Jones
PRINCIPAL SCRIBE

Countersigned ....
Nautical Assessor to THE RULER OF THE RAGING MAIN.

Dinner on Board

s.s. Ocean Monarch

S.S. Ocean Monarch
161 DAYS & 54,730 MILES LATER

During the Voyage She

MADE 31 CALLS
AT
16 DIFFERENT PORTS
IN
9 DIFFERENT COUNTRIES
AND
**CROSSED THE EQUATOR 6 TIMES
IN DOING SO**

It Was Great Having You Aboard With Us
NEVER HAVE SO FEW, DONE SO MUCH, FOR SO MANY

*Did a Brave and Courageous Deed
in boarding*

S.S. Ocean Monarch
on November 5th 1971 at Southampton

THE PRINTERS SHOP ON THE "EMPRESS OF ENGLAND"

People were surprised when you said that your job was Ship's Printer. We printed Menus, News Papers, Programmes, Bar Prices, Tour Tickets, as well as all the paperwork and forms to keep these floating cities going. And that was just the official things that had to be printed!

Fancy Dress Night
—
BUFFET SUPPER

Friday 17th July, 1970

s.s. Ocean Monarch

South China Sea

Shaw Savill Line

concert programme

programme for today

CUNARD

R.M.S. "Queen Elizabeth"
COMMODORE G. T. MARR, D.S.C., R.D., (Cr. R.N.R. Rtd.)

For Ship's Notices and Movie Programme — Please see reverse side of Programme

Suggested Dress for this evening — Formal

★   ★

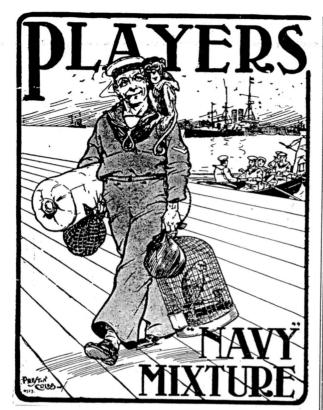

Visiting a Liner.

The spectacle of a great liner at the St. George's stage —whether arriving or departing—has attraction for everyone with the minutes to spare. Several of the steamship companies time their boats to leave in mid-afternoon ; and some great ship comes in or goes out practically every day of the week.

A visit to an Atlantic or other liner of the first class is certainly part of a Merseyside holiday. Thanks to a mutual arrangement between the Overhead Railway and the various Shipping Companies, it is now quite easy to visit a liner in dock without giving previous notice. The booking clerk at any Overhead station will issue, on request with a return ticket, a pass which will enable anyone to enter the Dock Estate and to go on board a specified ship. The Cunard, White Star, Canadian Pacific and other lines have arranged a system for visits. The dock station and the berth vary. These arrangements are for weekdays only. The best time for visits is in the early afternoon, as most of the ships lift their visitors' gangway about 5 p.m.

FACTS ILLUSTRATING THE MAGNITUDE OF THE DOCK SYSTEM.

No. of Docks	68
Total area of Dock Estate in Liverpool	1,335¾ acres
Water area in Docks	460 acres
Total length of Dock Quays	27½ miles
Total length of Graving Docks	10,450 feet
Warehouse Quays on Dock Estate	8,207 lineal feet
Tonnage of Ships entering and leaving Port	52 millions
Vessels paying Dock Tonnage and Harbour rates	18,000
Length of Dock Railways	79 miles
No. of loaded Railway wagons (1955)	227,929—2,169,681 tons
No. of Cranes (Hydraulic, Electric, Steam, Hand Runabout, Portable) capable of lifting 10 cwt. to 50 tons	446
Floating Cranes capable of lifting 25 to 200 tons	8

THE BUSES

LIVERPOOL TRANSPORT

ROUTE MAP

Price Sixpence

A Liverpool Corporation Passenger Transport Guide. Routes, fares, times and maps. This is from the days when everything as dependable. When an effort was made to give people a reliable service, something that they could count on. Alas those days have gone, and we can only look back with a sigh and a shake of the head. Wouldn't it be nice to know when a bus was going to run and even IF! it was going to run, and the fare to remain the same long enough to print a guide!

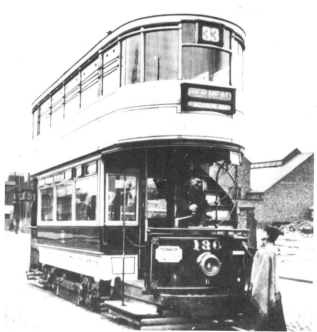

Here is a helpful idea. The last trams from all the outlying areas had a post box on the front, and at any stop you could post your card or letter. At the Pier Head a Post Office van would meet the trams and collect the post from the boxes, simple! Here is the number 33 just about to start off from Garston about 1924. The sign to the right of the driver's head would indicate that the Post Box was on that tram

The number 5 tram ran up Church Street, and up Smithdown Road to terminate at Manor Road in Woolton. When it was taken over by buses it started from South Castle Street. Can you make out the advert "You should live on Melbreck Estate, Allerton for Your Health" on the side of the tram?

A postcard of a Liverpool Corporation Tram dated 189 . If a tram was always full or they knew they were going to be busy, they hitched another carriage on to the back for the extra passengers. This picture was taken at Dingle getting ready to set off back to 'Town'.

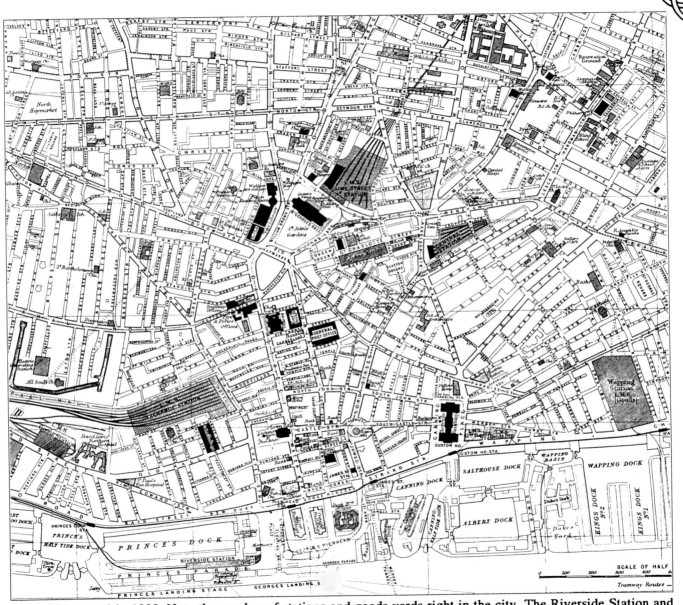

Central Liverpool in 1930. Note the number of stations and goods yards right in the city. The Riverside Station and the L. M. S. goods yard to the left, with Wapping Station and the goods depot on the right, as well as the Overhead.

A 1956 shot of the Pier Head and its mixture of trams and buses. The name Pier Head is an old 'nick name'. There was once a pier, a stones and rubble effort, that stuck out into the River, roughly where the Floating Road was. It was incorporated into the old Georges' Dock but the name Pier Head stuck.

They called these trams 'Baby Grands' and they were the ultimate in modern trams, and lasted right to the end. A 19A stands solitary on the first loop outside the Dock Office in 1956.

A postcard of the most photographed tram in Liverpool: the number 293 (A Baby Grand). It was painted white and marked 'Liverpool's Last Tram' and on the 14th September 1957 it was the Last Tram in the procession of trams travelling for the last time to the Pier Head.

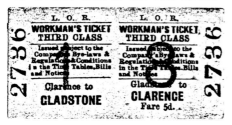

There was a railway station right down on the Princess Dock and trains met the Trans-Atlantic and Cruising liners. A train to London and a train to Harwich (for the Continent) met all the ships from New York and Montreal. Getting this train on to the main lines was a major headache, and it was decided to go for Edge Hill to join up with the Main Line. What an introduction to England some visitors must have received when they got off the boat and straight on to these trains. It went under the Overhead railway, then across and up the dock road following a man with a red flag, then through all the goods yards and sidings. Then, it went through a steep cutting and a 6 mile tunnel to emerge at Edge Hill and off on to the main line.

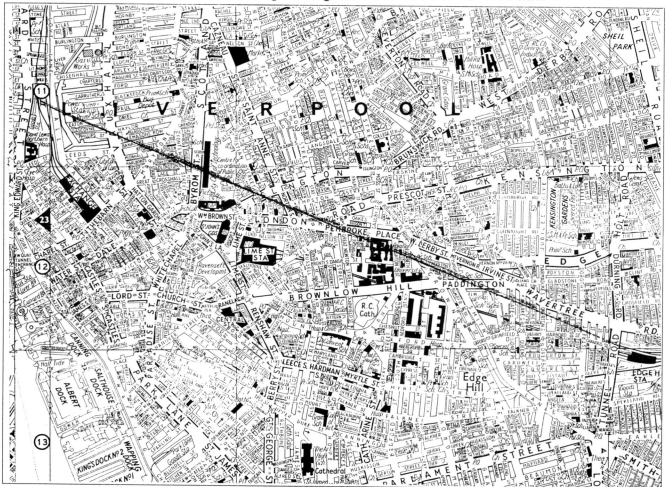

Including the cuttings the tunnel was seven miles long. This shows in pencil where it ran, and although it ceased to be used in 1971 I think most of it is still there. I wonder what they could do with it?

Even the Isle of Man boats had trains at the landing stage to meet them.

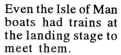

A compound loco stands waiting in a murky and atmospheric Exchange Station.
In the 50s we used to trainspot here — what excitement when the Glasgow–Liverpool train came in with a 'Clan' or 'Brit' on.

NEW PERIOD RETURN TICKETS
BY NIGHT TRAINS
— at a —
SPECIAL LOW FARE
EVERY NIGHT
— to —

24/9
RETURN

LONDON
(EUSTON)

24/9
RETURN

LIVERPOOL

(Lime Street) (dep.) †11-50 p.m.

RETURNING ANY NIGHT within 17 days from and including date of issue · from LONDON (EUSTON) 12-35 midnight. †10-45 p.m. Sundays.

ASHTON DAVIES, Chief Commercial Manager.

LONDON.

TOUR A.

† Outward Friday night, returning Saturday night.

		£	s.	d.
TRAIN.	Liverpool to London and return		16	0
DRIVE.	City of London, visiting Tower of London, and all principal Buildings and places of interest (3½ hours drive) (Approx.) (Guides can be provided at a cost of 12/6 per bus.)		3	0
MEALS.	(Approx.)		6	0
		£1	5	0

(† On other days the rail fare is 24/9.)

TOUR B.

† Outward Friday night, returning Saturday night.

		£	s.	d.
TRAIN.	Liverpool to London and return		16	0
DRIVE.	Kensington Gardens, Kew Gardens, Richmond, Twickenham, Hampton Court, returning via Roehampton, Barnes, Hammersmith, and Hyde Park Corner (3½ hours drive) (Approx.) (Guides can be provided at a cost of 12/6 per bus.)		3	0
MEALS.	(Approx.)		6	0
		£1	5	0

A British Rail advert for a day in London . . . and many took them up on their offers.

The last time a steam train came to Lime Street Station, in March, 1981. Pity it was a southern engine: Lord Nelson.

THE TUNNEL

In 1827 the Liverpool Mercury reported that a tunnel was being planned under the River Mersey and Brunel himself was asked to estimate and plan for an 'underground' crossing of the River Mersey from Liverpool. When it finally opened over 100 years later, in 1934, the Mersey Tunnel was the largest and longest undertaking of its kind in the world. At the time the plans were drawn up it was thought that a two tier tunnel was a MUST. The road on top, and a tramway below.

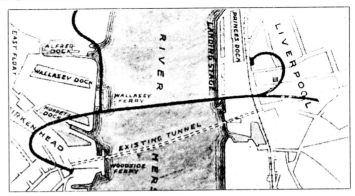

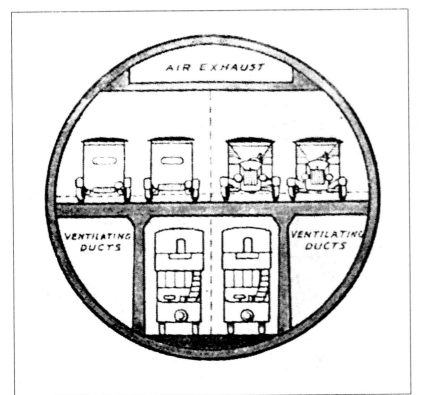

Section of Tunnel as originally planned, with double track for road vehicles above and tramway track below

For some time in 1913 the idea of a bridge across the river was put forward. In fact a bridge was proposed to go from behind the Museum in William Brown Street to Birkenhead (a total of 3,500 yards). But the idea of restricting the shipping with their tall masts, and then the start of the First World War finally put paid to this idea.

H.M. KING GEORGE V

TYPICAL SECTION UNDER RIVER

THE MERSEY TUNNEL, LIVERPOOL & BIRKENHEAD
UNDER THE RIVER MERSEY.
OPENED BY HIS MAJESTY THE KING.   (74)

G.269.

A card from the opening year of the tunnel. The whole of Merseyside was excited at this great event. Over 1,500 vehicles were carried by the ferries in 1932 and all this and more was expected to use the new tunnel.

Here is another early picture of the tunnel taken in 1935.

Almost before and after shots. A postcard from 1932 of work going on the tunnel, and a later one of the nearly completed tunnel.

THE MERSEY TUNNEL.

The Mersey Tunnel was officially opened by King George V on 18th July, 1934, and named "Queensway."

The main Liverpool entrance, "Kingsway," is situated in the Haymarket, and the auxiliary entrance, New Quay, is near the Pierhead. The Birkenhead main entrance, "King's Square," is at Chester Street, and the auxiliary entrance at Rendel Street. The Tunnel is always open.

The Main Tunnel is intersected for two lines of traffic in each direction.

Electro-matic signals operate at the junction of the auxiliary tunnels with the main one.

Extract from Official Regulations.

Strict compliance with these regulations will help to ensure your safety, as well as that of others.

Speeds.

Slow Lane. Minimum, 6 m.p.h. Maximum, 21 m.p.h.

Fast Lane. Minimum, 21 m.p.h. Maximum, 30 m.p.h.

Keep in Lane. - OVERTAKING PROHIBITED.

NO CROSSING WHITE LINES EXCEPT AS INDICATED AT JUNCTIONS OR AUTHORIZED BY A TUNNEL OFFICER.
KEEP 75 FEET APART.
SOUNDING HORN PROHIBITED.
HEADLIGHTS OUT IN TUNNEL.
KEEP IN GEAR. COASTING PROHIBITED.
OBSERVE AND OBEY TRAFFIC SIGNALS AND NOTICES.

Signal Lights. Red.-STOP. Amber.-CAUTION. Green.- PROCEED. GREEN ARROW at Liverpool Junction allows filtration to the left to New Quay exit.

If a "STOP YOUR ENGINE" signal is displayed, STOP YOUR ENGINE AT ONCE, and keep it stopped until signal is extinguished and traffic is allowed to resume.

PETROL REMINDER. See that you have sufficient petrol in the tank. Vehicles requiring tyre or wheel changes, or breaking down or running out of fuel, will be removed to the most convenient exit by the Tunnel breakdown wagon. The driver of any vehicle requiring to be so removed will be charged a fee equal to double its ordinary toll, in addition to the toll already paid. Proceed through the tunnel without stopping, unless prevented by traffic, traffic officers, traffic signals, or other unavoidable cause.

Use of branch tunnels is barred, or restricted, between 8.30 a.m. and 10 a.m., and 4.30 p.m. and 6.15 p.m. Monday to Friday.

Maximum height of vehicle loaded, 13 ft. 6 in.; maximum width of vehicle loaded, 9 ft.; maximum weight of vehicle loaded, 10 tons per axle. Drivers of vehicles of more than the above height or width, but not more than 16 ft. high, must get in touch by letter or telephone with the Traffic Manager, Georges Dock Bldgs., Liverpool 3, 'phone Central 1020, giving time of arrival so that arrangements can be made for them to be escorted.

No additional charge will be made for the Driver and other person or persons required by law to be carried on the vehicle or trailer.

Other persons conveyed in or on vehicles will be charged as follows:-

Children under 14 years of age		1d.
Other persons		2d.

	TOLL per vehicle.	Trailer- Addit'l. Charge per Trailer.
Motor Cars. (Taxed according to H.P.)		
Not exceeding 8 H.P.	1/-	1/-
Exceeding 8 H.P. but not exceeding 12 H.P.	1/6	1/6
Exceeding 12 H.P.	2/-	1/6
Motor Bicycle	6d.	-
Motor Bicycle & Side-Car	9d.	-
Motor Car (3 wheels - 2 seats)	1/-	-
Goods Vehicles. Not otherwise specified. (Unladen weight.)		
Not exceeding 1 ton	1/-	1/-
Exceeding 1 ton but not exceeding 30 cwts.	1/6	1/6
Exceeding 30 cwts. but not exceeding 2 tons	2/-	2/-
Exceeding 2 tons but not exceeding 4 tons	2/6	2/-
Exceeding 4 tons	2/6	2/6
Motor Tractors.	1/-	1/6
Hackney Vehicles. (Seating capacity, excluding Driver.)		
Not exceeding 6 persons	1/6	-
Exceeding 6 persons but not exceeding 8 persons	2/-	-
Exceeding 8 persons but not exceeding 14 persons	2/6	-
Exceeding 14 persons but not exceeding 26 persons	3/6	-
Exceeding 26 persons	5/-	-

PAYMENT OF TOLLS. The above tolls are payable to the Toll Collector before entering the tunnel.

When the tunnel was opened there were a lot of rules and regulations. "No going under 6 miles per hour". "No coasting" and they actually charged you according to horse power.

Opened Easter 1893 and the first ever to be operated by electricity. The Overhead Railway was 13 miles long and it boasted in the years after the war "We run even in the THICKEST Fog!" It really was practical, yet it was magic. It was said to have been inspired by the New York Overhead Steam Railway. But it was a rare combination of workers transport, and a tourist attraction.

THE LIVERPOOL OVERHEAD RAILWAY

A SPLENDID VIEW OF THE DOCKS & RIVER

FIRST & FASTEST
ELECTRIC
(OVERHEAD) RAILWAY
IN THE WORLD.

RAPID AND FREQUENT SERVICE
OF SALOON CARS AT
CHEAP FARES

Affording Magnificent Panoramic View
OF THE LIVERPOOL DOCKS
6½ miles in extent
AND THE RIVER MERSEY.

Car number 27 comes into the station on the Overhead Railway in 1950, Tate & Lyle's shows behind.

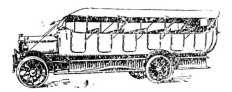

To Racecourses, Regattas, the Countryside and the Seaside by elegant Motor Coach

◆◆◆

If you are over 50 and a Scouser there is one thing that will bring a smile to your face or a long lost look to your eyes — 'The Overhead Railway' or 'Dockers Umbrella' as it was fondly known.

Down at the South and the original end of the line, Herculaneum Dock Station, now just a shed in this photograph from 1896 and the line on the left going towards the Dingle tunnel.

One old guard on the Overhead swears that he knew of a dog which accompanied his master to work at Herculaneum Docks and came home by itself with a ticket bought that morning, tucked into its collar.

The Overhead Railway survived the War and this 1947 card shows a train heading south with the Dock & Liver Buildings behind.

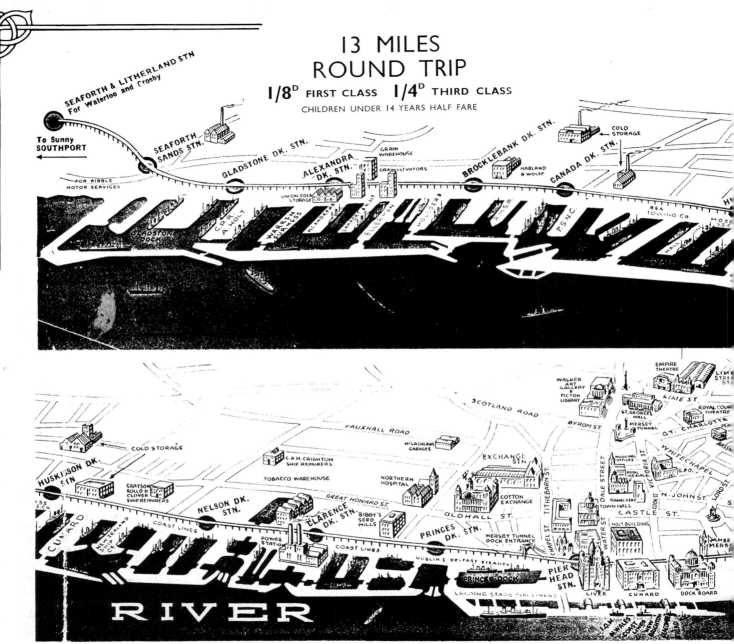

13 MILES
ROUND TRIP

1/8ᴰ FIRST CLASS **1/4ᴰ** THIRD CLASS

CHILDREN UNDER 14 YEARS HALF FARE

SEAFORTH & LITHERLAND STN
For Waterloo and Crosby

To Sunny
SOUTHPORT

FOR RIBBLE
MOTOR SERVICES

SEAFORTH
SANDS STN.

GLADSTONE DK. STN.

ALEXANDRA
DK. STN.

GRAIN
WAREHOUSE

GRAIN ELEVATORS

BROCKLEBANK DK. STN.

HARLAND
& WOLFF

CANADA DK. STN.

COLD
STORAGE

UNION COLD
STORAGE

C.P.R.
A. HOLT

BOSTON

WARREN
CURLESS

ELDER DEMPSTER

ELLERMAN

HOLDERS

R.M.S.P.

P.S.N.C.

REA
TOWING CO.

MOSS
S.S.C.

HALL LINE

COLD STORAGE

HUSKISSON DK.
STN.

GRAYSON
ROLLO &
CLOVER
SHIP REPAIRERS

C & H. CRICHTON
SHIP REPAIRERS

TOBACCO WAREHOUSE

McLACHLANS
GARAGES

NORTHERN
HOSPITAL

VAUXHALL ROAD

SCOTLAND ROAD

EXCHANGE
STN.

COTTON
EXCHANGE

OLDHALL ST.

WALKER
ART
GALLERY
&
PICTON
LIBRARY

BYROM ST.

ST. GEORGES
HALL

MERSEY
TUNNEL

EMPIRE
THEATRE

LIME
STREET
ST.

LIME ST.

ROYAL COURT
THEATRE

GT. CHARLOTTE

WHITECHAPEL

MUNICIPAL
OFFICES

ROYAL
INSURANCE

G.P.O.

N. JOHN ST.

LORD ST.

CASTLE ST.

NELSON DK.
STN.

CLARENCE
DK. STN.

BIBBY'S
SEED
MILLS

GREAT HOWARD ST.

PRINCES
DK. STN.

POWER
STATION

MERSEY TUNNEL
DOCK ENTRANCE

CHAPEL ST.

TITHEBARN ST.

DALE STREET

VICTORIA ST.

COOK ST.

TUNNEL VENT
TOWN HALL

HOLT BUILDING

CUNARD

NEW ZEALAND
SHIPPING CO.

COAST LINES

COAST LINES

DUBLIN & BELFAST STEAMERS

PRINCES DOCK

LANDING STAGE FOR LINERS

PIER
HEAD
STN.

LIVER   CUNARD   DOCK BOARD

I.O.M.
N. WALES
COAST LINES

RIVER

Don't peep. See if you can remember the names of the stations starting north from Litherland.

Price TWO PENCE.

LIVERPOOL OVERHEAD RAILWAY

DESCRIPTIVE
MAP AND GUIDE
OF THE
RAILWAY AND DOCKS

For full particulars of Educational Tours, School Parties, Works Outing, Etc., apply to :
H. Maxwell Rostron, *General Manager and Engineer*, Hargreaves Building, 5, Chapel Street, Liverpool, 3
TELEPHONE CENTRAL 5134

THE BEST VIEW
OF THE DOCKS & LINERS

The Roman Catholic Cathedral is a striking and imposing building, but it wasn't planned to turn out like it has. In 1930 there was a pro-Catherdral in Hawke Street that had been there since 1812. Dedicated to St. Nicholas it consisted of only a chancel and nave. In 1932 a scheme to build a new cathedral on a site at the top of Brownlow Hill began. Sir Edward Lutyens was engaged as architect, and this was how the building was meant to turn out. Described as three great triple porches and a sequence of barrel vaults to carry a great dome.

A rare postcard. Sold to raise funds for the new R.C. Cathedral which was to be built in memory of Archbishop Whiteside. The card was Lutyens' vision of the finished work and had been drawn by him. 1937 saw the opening of the chapels in the crypt then along came the war in 1939 and all work stopped. The plans were taken up again in 1949 and Sir Adrian G. Scott was asked to finish it after Sir Edwin Lutyens died. Even as late as 1955 this is how it was to turn out. Then a change of plans, and architect-(Sir Frederick Gibberd) and the 'Space Ship' is what Liverpool ended up with.

Have you been doing what you were told on page eleven and keeping a close eye on the pictures that included the Cathedral? No other city has had such a magnificent edifice growing in its midst for so long.

This was how the young 21-year-old architect saw the finished building when he was appointed in 1903.

The Lady Chapel Liverpool

In 1900 when Dr. Chavasse was appointed the second Bishop of Liverpool, he formed a Committee who raised £325,000. and plans were put in hand for a Cathedral worthy of the City and its people.

On July 19th 1904 King Edward VII laid the foundation stone. In 1910 the Lady Chapel was completed. Here is a postcard from 1912 showing Lady Chapel which was used as a church until 1924. In 1911 the architect went to the Committee and persuaded them to change the plans to only one high tower instead of the original two smaller towers. The 1914-18 War certainly slowed work down through loss of workers going to War. In July 1924 King George V & Queen Mary were present when the Choir and Eastern Transept were consecrated.

Anyone looking to the female movement could do a lot worse than make a note of the names on the window and try to find out a little about each of them. Kitty Wilkinson, Alice Marval, Mother Cecile & Louisa Stewart among the others worth looking into.

The famous 'Notable Women Window' in the Lady Chapel. A 1910 postcard published by Rasmus R. Madsen of Anfield shows: Queen Victoria, Elizabeth Fry, Susanna Wesley, Catherine Gladstone, Elizabeth Browning among the other worthy ladies shown in this Window. The window along with the Staircase Window were given by the Liverpool Diocesan Girls' Friendly Society.

Hope Street not only links the two Cathedrals and religions, it has at one end the quickest Cathedral to be built, taking only five years, and at the other the slowest, taking 72 years to complete.

The staircase window

The Cathedral, Liverpool.

A 1932 postcard showing the work going ahead on the Great Central Tower. It was 1949 before this third and final part was started, nearly 50 years on from when it was first began.

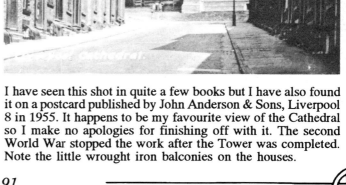

I have seen this shot in quite a few books but I have also found it on a postcard published by John Anderson & Sons, Liverpool 8 in 1955. It happens to be my favourite view of the Cathedral so I make no apologies for finishing off with it. The second World War stopped the work after the Tower was completed. Note the little wrought iron balconies on the houses.

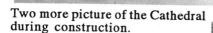

Two more picture of the Cathedral during construction.

What is a Seaman ?

Between the security of childhood and the insecurity of second childhood, we find a fascinating group of humanity that come in assorted shapes, sizes, weights and states of soberiety : they are found on ships, ashore, in love, in passenger accomodation, but always in debt.

Girl's love them, towns tolerate them, shipping companies support them, and calabooses all over the world provid them with overnight shelter.

A seaman is easiness with a deck of cards, brave with a stomach full of hooch and the world's best buyers of "Man Only" and other such artistic literature.

He has the energy of a tortoise, brains of an idiot, yarns of an old sea-dog and the slyness of a fox.

Some of his interests are women, girls, females and the opposite sex. His dislikes are work, answering letters, the " Old Man," inspections, the horrible call of "Turn to" and ship's food.

No-one else can cram into a back pocket his Seaman's Book, Union Card, Identification Book, a photo of his wife & his girl friend 3 unanswered letters, a comb, crushed packet of fags, a train ticket, what is left of his pay-off and the odd cruzeiro, peso, peseta, escuda, dollar or franc.

A seaman is an amazing creature, you can lock him out of your home but not your heart, you can wipe him off your writing list but not your mind.

He is your seagoing life, your only one and only good-for-nothing bundle of worry, and all your shattered dreams are insignificant when a seaman looks at you with those bleary, bloodshot eyes and gives his lop-sided and sometimes toothless grin and says "I'm home love."

THE LANGUAGE OF STAMPS

I came across a postcard around 1900 with "Please don't place the stamp upside down". I wondered about that and started to look for upside down stamps on the back of my postcards. I found one or two, but I also found some in other corners, and some stuck on at odd angles.

Then, in a book on the social history of Britain, I found the full explanation. Like S.W.A.L.K. (Sealed With a Loving Kiss) and I.T.A.L.Y. (I Trust and Love You) on the back of envelopes, it was a code. This 'stamp code' was normally used by courting couples in late Victorian and Edwardian times when the postcard craze was at its peak. Because postcards were so open and easily read by all, a 'hidden message' language grew up.

It was not 'the done thing' for a young lady to beg a young man to write to her, but if she put an upside down stamp in the opposite corner she could get her message across.

Lovers could always use their own version of this code to do their courting and wooing under their parents noses. You must remember that everyone sent postcards to everyone else. Cousins and friends wrote weekly, or even more often to each other. There were no phones, so postcards were the chatty way of keeping in touch. A postcard from a young man or a young lady was usual an acceptable but a letter was a serious business so the courting couple stuck to postards with the hidden message in the stamps.

I wonder if the next time I pay my electricity bill I stick the stamp sideways in the bottom left corner they may take the hint?

Top, Left-Hand Corner				Top, Right-Hand Corner			
I hate you	Good-bye for the present	My heart belongs to another and can never be yours	I love you	My heart is given to another write to me no more	Do you love me, dearest	A kiss	Business

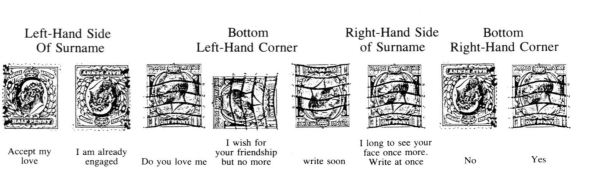

Left-Hand Side Of Surname		Bottom Left-Hand Corner		Right-Hand Side of Surname		Bottom Right-Hand Corner	
Accept my love	I am already engaged	Do you love me	I wish for your friendship but no more	write soon	I long to see your face once more. Write at once	No	Yes

CRICKET
A TALE OF HUMBLE LIFE.

BY

SILAS K. HOCKING

Author of "Her Benny," "Sea Waif," etc., etc., etc.

" I'll carry you as far as I can."

LONDON
FREDERICK WARNE AND CO
AND NEW YORK.

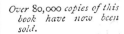

OTHER BOOK CLEARANCE CENTRES

Unit 28a, Town Square Shopping Centre, Oldham, OL1 1XD.
Tel: 0161 627 5244.

Unit 6, Marketgate Shopping Centre, Wigan, WN1 1JS.
Tel: 01942 829499.

Unit 2-8, Fishergate Centre, Preston, PH1 8HJ.
Tel: 01772 884846.

27-28, Dawson Way, St. John's Shopping Precinct, Liverpool, L1 1LH.
Tel: 0151 708 5176.

7 The Mall, Millgate Centre Bury, BL9 9QQ.
Tel: 0161 763 5700.
